IDENTITY CRISIS

Jeffrey D. Harris

Parted Waters

For more books from Parted Waters visit

www.partedwaters.net

Holy Bible, New Living Translation, copyright © ©1996, 2004, 2007, 2013, 2015 by Tyndale House Foundation. Used by permission of Tyndale House Publishers Inc., Carol Stream, Illinois 60188. All rights reserved.

Scripture quotations marked (NLT) are taken from the Holy Bible, New Living Translation, copyright © 1996, 2004, 2007, 2013, 2015 by Tyndale House Foundation. Used by permission of Tyndale House Publishers, Inc., Carol Stream, Illinois 60188. All rights reserved.

Scripture quotations marked HCSB are taken from the Holman Christian Standard Bible®, Copyright © 1999, 2000, 2002, 2003, 2009 by Holman Bible Publishers. Used by permission. Holman Christian Standard Bible®, Holman CSB®, and HCSB® are federally registered trademarks of Holman Bible Publishers.

This book came from a sermon series that I was allowed to share while serving at The House Memphis church.

While there are many other resources about this subject. I believe this book will speak to you in a way other books have not.

Special Thanks to Mary Kane for her help with editing the book. She was amazing and a longtime friend.

Identity Crisis

We are all a bit different. We are all a bit off, as they say. We all have our unique way of looking at the world. In the following chapters we will look at obstacles that hinder our God-given Identity.

The goal of this book is to encourage you to be the best you can be, to be everything God has called you to be, and to do amazing things.

Sometimes we are afraid to be ourselves.

Sometimes we are told we should be ourselves.

Sometimes we just don't know who we are.

Read on and find yourself.

There is beauty

inside of you

waiting to emerge.

Contents

1. Who am I   Pg 1

2. Who are you   Pg 7

3. Lost Identity   Pg 13

4. Denying Identity   Pg 19

5. Suppressed Identity   Pg 23

6. Hidden Identity   Pg 29

7. Resented Identity   Pg 35

8. Skeptical Identity   Pg 41

9. Rejected Identity   Pg 45

10. Best Identity   Pg 49

Chapter 1

Who am I?

I am Jeffrey David Harris by birth, second child of Kathie and John David. Throughout my life, I have had several identities. Some of these identities have been good and some have been harsh. I have had to deal with each one in one way or another.

"Now here's everything people have said about me, both the good and the bad."

1. Son: My first identity was son, grandson, and preemie.
2. Hopeless: The doctors said there was no hope, I would be dead by morning or the next day.
3. Defended: My grandmother made a huge fuss and refused to let the doctors quit on me.
4. Survivor: Through God's help, I recovered and grew into an almost normal person.

5. Dyslexic: At five, I got a new name. I became FFEJ. I wrote my name backwards and no one knew why. To the family it was funny at first.

6. Friend: I met my amazing neighborhood friends, Scott and Thad.

7. Dreamer: In third grade, we had an Author come into the class and tell us about writing. Despite not being able to read well, I gained another identity. I wanted to be a writer. Dreaming was right. I could hardly read, and I wanted to write books. Maybe I was insane instead.

8. Stupid: It didn't matter that I had dyslexia. It didn't matter why I wrote backwards. It didn't matter that I could read. I just couldn't read out loud. To all my classmates, I was stupid.

9. Failure: I found myself in a new class in the same school doing fifth grade over again. There is no way to hide that fact. There is no way to escape that. There is no way to convince fifth graders of anything other than what they see. A failure.

10. Scout: When a boy has a hard time fitting in, join the Boy Scouts. I jest. While I didn't add to my friendships outside the troop, I did make lifelong friendships and went on amazing adventures.

11. Accomplished: I found I was good at things and was able to succeed at activities by earning merit badges. In fact, I earned a ton of them and made rank quickly.

12. Eagle Scout: I completed the program and discovered many interests I was good at. Still to this day, I am considered an Eagle Scout.

13. Junior High: Continued to struggle in school. Once again, I was called a failure. The teachers even joined in the mockery. One time, I had a teacher in front of the class tell me that I would never amount to anything.

14. Bullied: I was beat up in the stairwells of my junior high. I was called names and laughed at. Yet, I still had a few great friends like Lee and Scott, but for the most part was still a failure to most.

15. Too Small: Ninth grade came with a rough start and an amazing finish. First, I was too small and rode the bench in football, but I loved to run laps.

16. Runner: The high school track coach saw me and recruited me to run with the big kids in January. And I loved it. I was good at it. I made the varsity team as a sophomore, as well as new friends.

17. Schmangy: It was running cross country that I got this new nickname. This would be an identity that would make a major change in my life. It meant acceptance. The funny thing is the name came from a nerdy character that Eugene Levy played. Once I was given the name, I felt cooler than I ever had before.

18. Goody 2 Shoes: Despite my new circle of friends, I was not invited to most parties, since I wasn't going to join in with the so-called fun. I also learned that most girls don't like nice guys (the good ones do).

19. Squid, Sailor, Petty Officer Harris: The Navy was the next big change. Not only did I move away from home, I was really good at being a sailor. I excelled as an Aircraft Electrician. I was good at school. Really good. I even came back to teach at the A-School. I became a teacher. I was good at something that wasn't just running.

20. Ace/Deuce President: Despite being younger than my fellow teachers, I became a teacher my second tour. Most are on their fourth, with more experience. As I was saying, I was voted in as our club's president. I was voted for something by my peers. This is something that has never happened before.

21. Puppeteer: I found Raleigh Assembly of God and learned to serve in the church. I joined the puppet team

and found a new skill. I excelled once again. I quickly became known as Mr. Jeff to all the kids.

22. Weird: With puppets and drama team events, I found a great outlet for my weirdness.

23. Singer: After a call from a friend of a friend, I had an audition with the Bluff City Quartet. They needed a bass singer. I made it and joined the group. I am still singing bass today.

24. Author: Today, I am still not good at a lot of things, but I have had success after success. Looking all the way back to third grade, my dreams were fulfilled when I finished my first book. It was a devotional and I sold over 300 copies. Not bad for selling them out of my car.

As you can see, I had many Identities. I still do. I even have many more. Dad, Husband, Boss, Elder, Christian, etc. We all have multiple identities. It is up to us to decide whether we hold on to the bad ones or grab hold of the good ones with everything we have.

I didn't let what was going on in Junior High stop me from going on amazing camping adventures in Scouts. I also didn't let it stop me from earning merit badges. During one of the worst years of my life, I stood tall and proud as Mr. Manson pinned on my Eagle Scout medal. I also didn't let the big identity as a Dyslexic stop me from writing several books, including this one.

Before I move on, I must talk about the God-given Identity. The identity that cannot be changed or erased by anyone else.

I am FORGIVEN.

I have humbled myself and asked Jesus to forgive me. I believed in his power over sin. I became a Christ follower at an early age. God made the difference. I can't say I would have had half the success I have had without Him.

John 3:15
..So that everyone who believes in Him will have eternal life.
HCSB

Questions:

1. What's the identity God has given to you?

   _____

   _____

2. Have you been marked with a negative identity?

   _____

   _____

3. Do you believe God can help you overcome any negative identity?

   _____

4. Have you overcome identities others have put upon you?

   _____

5. Who did Jesus Die for? _____

6. Are you an everyone? _____

Step one; is accepting that we are one of the ones Jesus died for and we are worthy. Even in our unworthiness we are worthy.

Thoughts:

Chapter 2

Who are you?

Who do you think you are? What do you think identifies you as a person?

1. Mother or Father
2. Dallas or Bama fan
3. Drama Queen or Work Out Queen
4. White or Black
5. Cool or Nerd
6. Republican or Democrat
7. Singer or Wall Flower
8. Single Parent or Widow
9. Divorced or Lonely

Identity can be taken from a status, your job, or a hobby. It could be an activity that uses up all our free time. For some of you, that all-consuming activity is motherhood.

Who do others say you are?

1. Man or Woman
2. Divorced or Single
3. Poor or Rich
4. Ugly or Pretty
5. Health Nut or Fat
6. Funny or Too Serious
7. Annoying or Shy
8. Athletic or Lazy
9. Sick or Handicapped
10. Partier

There are people in our lives that will only ever see us in one role. Therefore, our identity to them is from only a single source. It may be from work, whether the company or your position. When I was in the Navy, I was a Petty Officer. Now, I am the warehouse guy at Barnhart.

If it is a hobby, there will be people that only know you as a biker, kayaker, tennis player, or bird watcher. It could also be from an organization or your position within the organization.

It also could be your personality or the way you act. Like flighty, airhead, bossy, freak, or shy.

The thing about these limited contact identities is they only see you in one context. This makes their opinion of you, whether good or bad, an incomplete opinion. Thus, you should only take a small amount of value in their opinion.

As a singer, I run into people that have only heard me sing. Yet they constantly give me way too much credit. I have had them say I must be a great husband or father. While I am flattered, they have made a judgement with very limited knowledge. I know some great singers that are total jerks. I guess they can see a glimpse of my character, so the judgement is not totally blind.

This same type of judgement can be negative also.

Jesus had the same judgement projected on him, even still to this day. People with limited exposure defining who he is. I believe he was crucified for not being what people expected him to be. He was supposed to come as a warrior king to take down the Romans and set up a permanent Jewish Kingdom. The Bible tells us exactly why he came.

John 3:17
"For God did not send his son into the world that he might condemn the world, but that the word might be saved through him." HCSB

Mark 10:45 (ESV)
"For even the Son of Man came not to be served but to serve, and to give his life as a ransom for many."

He came to save the entire world, not just the Jews. He did not come to rule over the world. He came to serve it. Even though we know he has every right to rule, that was not the purpose of this earthly visit.

Jesus knew he was being mis-identified. He used this knowledge to set up Peter for a quote that would change everything.

> *Matt 16:13-16*
>
> *"…He asked his disciples, "Who do people say that the Son of Man is?" And they said, "Some say John the Baptist; others, Elijah; still others, Jeremiah or one of the prophets."*
>
> *"But you," He asked them, "who do you say that I am?"*
>
> *Simon Peter answered, "You are the Messiah, the Son of the living God!" HCSB*

It was the revelation from the Holy Spirit. God reveals his true identity to us. He also reveals what our identity is. He knows who we really are, which includes who he designed us to be. This is a simple statement that is easier to say than to believe for ourselves.

The revelation of our identity comes from listening to the Holy Spirit. This cannot be done without reading God's Word. We must read the Bible to open our eyes to who we are. We just may find our identity isn't what we thought at all, or that it has been changed. We can see an example of this if we keep reading through verses 17 and 18.

> *"And Jesus responded, "Simon son of Jonah, you are blessed because flesh and blood did not reveal this to you, but My Father in heaven. And I also say to you that you are Peter, and on this rock, I will build My church…"*

He gave the hot-head disciple a new name: Peter the Rock. He gave several other people new names to set their purpose. When we ask for Jesus to enter our heart, we get a new life and our identity changes forever.

By the end of this book, I believe you will be more comfortable in your new identity.

Questions:

1. What is your favorite identity of Jesus?

   _____

2. How did people underestimate Jesus?

   _____

   _____

   _____

3. Name an identity, others have given you? _____

   _____

   _____

4. Name four identities you currently have? (Good or Bad)

   _____

   _____

5. What identity is in you, that most people have not seen?

   _____

   _____

Getting to know Jesus is essential for us to grow into who we are meant to be.

Thoughts:

Chapter 3

Lost Identity

We are at risk of losing our identity when we get distracted by life. This distraction can come from a multitude of places: home, work, church.

Any time we take our eyes off the prize, so to speak. When we stop living in the identity we were designed for or the identity that God has for us. We can lose it when we are right where we are supposed to be but lose sight of who we are in the busyness of life.

Lam 3:17-18
"My soul has been deprived of peace; I have forgotten what happiness is. Then I thought: My future is lost, as well as my hope from the Lord." HCSB

I have even seen it happen at church. Ministries that have great programs and helping many people, but it is not where God wants you to serve. We can justify our involvement because of the other servers or just because of the work that needs to be done. We don't let go, because of guilt; others convince us it is the place for us.

Guilt is a great motivator at church. Just because you feel guilty does not mean God is speaking to you. Guilt can keep us in a place we shouldn't be for years. If we get into these places, we can easily lose sight of our identity. There are times when we started out in a ministry and it was exactly where God placed us. Then the time comes, and God nudges us to move on, and we don't. There are so many ways to get ourselves into places we shouldn't be.

I know a young man that was not only a regular attender of church, he also served in ministry. Once he went off to college, and away from the positive environment of church, he drifted away. He had some health issues on top of the pressures of college, and soon lost contact with his church friends and church altogether. While there is still hope for him, he currently lives with a big part of his identity lost.

We can drive ourselves into places, but sometimes it is just life that drags us down.

The path we get on as young adults can lead to this loss. We leave high school knowing who we are and where we want to go. Then things don't go as smooth as we had planned. Within the search to take our identity to the next level, we get bogged down with work. Not just work, but we get loaded down with school, and socializing. We find ourselves very busy. This busyness continues day after day and month after month. Before we know it, we are wondering who we are and how we got where we ended up.

Some of you didn't have any troubles in your early adult years. The identity didn't start to fade away until kids came along. We embrace this new identity: moms and dads. We put everything we have into being parents and working hard to provide.

Our free time activities change to changing diapers. Both moms and dads find the new identities overwhelming. So much so they miss sight of the dreams and identities they were once convinced was their future.

Let me preface this by saying, for so many being a mother or father is exactly the identity that makes them complete. I want to look at how life can get in the way of the path God has for us.

Like any overwhelming life change, it is very difficult to stay on track. Basically, life happens. The day to day grind makes us go numb to life itself. We don't realize for a long time that we have let our calling or vision slip away. This loss causes depression, anger, and a sense of hopelessness.

Work is a great way to lose your identity. While for some of us, work was a place where our identity came out as we thrived. I have seen many people take jobs they shouldn't have taken, just for the paycheck.

Raises and promotions can be harmful. In the quest for the money, we can forget all about our identity. Maybe it isn't forgetting about it. Perhaps it is pursuing the wrong identity. Where it can be harmful is when someone moves into a position they are not suited for.

We need to put ourselves in positions that we can be a success in. Even though some of the proper changes will be challenging, the proper moves result in success.

I have a guy that was given to me a few years back in the attempt to give him a better job. He was a great employee. He had a great attitude. He did not have the aptitude. The position required mechanical skills. If you don't know, mechanical aptitude is something that cannot be taught. Much like hearing tones, it is something that we are born with or not. If someone is born tone deaf, they can't be taught to hear tones. Once he was placed in the new job doing preventive maintenance and using tools, his never-ending smiling face stopped smiling. Every day became stressful. The joy of work was washed away by tasks he had no idea how to do.

His story had a happy ending. We were able to get him back into a job that he loved and was perfectly designed for. That job is a gate guard. He is fantastic at it. When he is not at work, everyone knows it, because his replacements are never as good.

On paper; it would appear that a mechanic job would be the better job, with more pay and more prestige. The truth was he was, not good at the job, so he was miserable. The day he was put back at the gate, his never-ending smile was back. While he stands in the cold and rain to check in trucks, he has a joyful smile greeting everyone who passes through the gate.

His identity was lost by someone else's ideas. How many of us have found ourselves in the same situation? Placed somewhere we can't possibly be satisfied. There will be times when God places us into these positions to teach us something. In any case, these times are temporary.

Prayer is the best thing to do during these times of lost identity; for God to show a way out, to provide a way out. The way out may be drastic. It could be quitting a good job. It may be applying for a new job within the company. It may be just a new attitude until the next step in life comes along.

Regardless of the reasoning for the lost identity, God knows how to find it. Step one is realizing the identity is lost. This can take years to discover. Step two is looking to God for help. He knows where you are. He knows how you got there. More importantly, he knows how to get out of it. There were times when the only thing that had to change, was my attitude.

The thing to remember is it won't be lost forever.

Psalms 16:11
"You reveal the path of life to me; in Your presence is abundant joy; in Your right hand are eternal pleasures." HCSB

Questions:

1. What is your biggest distractions in your world?
   _____

2. What identity have you lost?
   _____
   _____
   _____

3. Do you believe God can help you find it?
   _____

4. What identity is worth looking for?
   _____

Jesus is the finder of lost things. Sheep, Coins, and Us. He can help you find what is lost in you.

Thoughts:

Chapter 4

Denying Identity

The Jonah Effect

Denying our identity is more common than you may think. It is when a person refuses to move into the position that God has set up for them or doesn't allow themselves to grow. Sometimes it is an identity they are openly running from or have simply closed off their heart to.

Fear is the major contributor to closing off our hearts from God. In the church, we close off our heart to keep God from leading us to the unknown.

Exodus 14:13
"Don't be afraid. Stand firm and see the Lord's salvation. He will provide for you today…" HCSB

Psalms 56:3
"When I am afraid, I will trust you." HCSB

I can't count all the men I have prayed for that have said they were called into ministry, that quit as soon as it got tough. Shortly thereafter, they aren't even in church anymore. For the longest time, I couldn't figure it out. How could they have had such a clear call from God only to fall away completely? I knew they were running from God.

The natural response to God when he sets us on a path that is paved with difficult stones is to run. It's the Jonah effect.

We want the title.

We want the position.

We don't always want the job.

We are all at risk of reacting the same way. As soon as the path God has put us on isn't what we expected, we want to quit. Trouble is, even when we quit, the calling is still there. The Holy Spirit reminds us of this every time we walk into the church. To avoid the guilt, we stop going.

The second part of the Jonah Effect: The Holy Spirit isn't only reminding us at church. This is why Jonah ran, as if he could get away from God. The farther he ran, the worse life got. On the ship, he tried hard to deny the calling God had for him.

Jonah wanted to be a prophet. He wanted to be respected. Everything was going along great until God told him to go to Nineveh.

The third part of the Jonah Effect: Jonah got bitter. He developed Resented Identity. Even after he delivered God's message and saved the entire city, he still wasn't happy. God wasn't doing anything the way he thought God should. Jonah got mad and sulked.

Every one of us finds our self on the edge when we try to follow God's calling. Inevitably, His plan is way different than what we planned.

We deny our identity when we say to ourselves, 'maybe it wasn't God calling me.' This is the lie of the Devil most of the time.

It is important that we stay in God's word and pray through the tough times to ensure we are on the right path. I find myself not wanting to read the Bible or even pray when I know that I am doing something I shouldn't be doing.

Just because you are having a hard time doesn't mean you are not on the right path. On the flip side, just because things are going smooth doesn't mean you are on the right path either.

We can't let our circumstances influence us into denying who we are and who we are meant to be. We must accept our identity and ask God to show us the path we need to be on. Pride blocks the way; humility paves the way.

We can also find ourselves denying our identity because of sin. Maybe we have even said to ourselves, "I used to be called…" Or "I used to think I was going to…" But the guilt of sin has us denying that the path God had us on is still there.

We are made righteous through Jesus, which means we can get back on that path.

God isn't giving up on you, so don't give up on God.

Psalms 25:4 (NLT)
Show me the right path, O Lord: point out the road for me to follow.

Questions:

1. Have you felt like Jonah, when God asked you to do something?
   _____

2. What was it you were asked to do?
   _____
   _____

3. What is the main thing in your life that holds you back from ministry or serving?
   _____

4. What do you feel like God wants you to do next?
   _____
   _____

5. Do you need a fresh start or a new beginning in Christ?
   _____

Jesus is all about new beginnings. His mercy is new every day. No matter where you are right now in your life. God is still ready to use you in amazing ways. Reach out and grasp hold of everything you can get from God to do the good works he has called you to do.

Thoughts:

Chapter 5

Suppressed Identity

Two of our biggest Bible heroes were suppressed by family. Both of their families laughed at them, especially when they spoke about it.

Joseph was the second youngest of twelve children. His father was Jacob, the famous grandson of Abraham.

On a side note, Jacob - like his grandfather - had his name changed by God. God changed Jacob's name to Israel. Abraham is known as the father of Israel. Jacob is the one who had the 12 sons that formed the twelve tribes.

Jacob had more than one wife, which never goes well. Joseph's mother was the one Jacob was in love with. You can read in Genesis how he was forced to marry Rachel's sisters before he could marry her. In addition to Joseph being born to Jacob's favorite wife, Rachel, the Bible also tells us it was because he was old when Joseph was born.

Joseph's stepbrothers hated him. This hatred escalated when Jacob gave Joseph a coat of many colors. But what put them over the top to the point of taking action to kill him was the dream.

The dream went as follows.

Genesis 37:7 "There we were, binding sheaves of grain in the field. Suddenly my sheaf stood up, and your sheaves gathered around it and bowed down to my sheaf." HCSB

Joseph would one day become the wisest person in all of Egypt. But on that morning, he did not show wisdom. He told his brothers.

This was the beginning of God's plan to use Joseph. Yes, even the act of telling his brothers. Please read the entire story in Genesis.

Joseph was sold into slavery by his brothers. This took Joseph to Egypt. As a slave he had several hardships. This included getting thrown into prison. Then he interpreted the Pharaoh's dream and was made a governor.

God took him from the hated son of God's chosen family to the savior of Egypt and his family. It was his plan to store up food to prepare for coming famine. As a result, the brothers that hated him were saved by him and they bowed down to him.

The brothers thought they could stop God's plan to use the person they hated most. But God used them to start the process to fulfill the prophecy.

The second person that was mocked by his brothers was also mocked by his father. In fact, he was mocked by everyone until the miracle happened. This person wasn't even a grown-up. He was a shepherd boy. He was the youngest son of Jesse.

The Lord sent the prophet Samuel to anoint a new king. King Saul had turned away from God, so God was looking for a replacement. Samuel know the next king was to come from Jesse. Jesse was super excited and knew he had the best sons around. Naturally Jesse thought it was one of his older sons, who had grown into fine young men. But as Samuel looked them over, none of them were right. So, he asked Jesse if he had another son.

I can't help but think this story inspired the story of Cinderella.

Jesse replied with reservation. The only son that was left was his son David, and he was way out in the field. He is hardly worth waiting for. Samuel said he would be glad to wait. I can imagine Jesse trying to talk Samuel into one of the other sons while they waited. As soon as Samuel saw David, he knew this was the one God had sent him to find. He wasted no time in anointing him with oil, marking him as the new King.

He was marked as the new king. You would think his life would change. But it didn't. As soon as Samuel left, David was sent back out into the fields.

It wasn't long before war with the Philistines broke out and Jesse's three older sons went off to defend Israel. One day Jesse sent David to the battle front with food for his sons. David arrived and heard the giant Goliath taunting Israel. David began to ask the Israelite soldiers why no one was going to stop this horrible giant. This did not make him any friends. When he volunteered to fight Goliath, his brothers told him to go home.

It is not clear why Saul let David fight. I think it may have been just to prevent fighting himself. David never doubted God's ability to kill this giant if someone would go. So, he knew God would use him because no one else was willing.

I have found in my life that just being willing and having faith is all we need for God to use us in a miracle.

As you know, God did help David and with a mere stone, he defeated the giant. David's life still wasn't easy but had many challenges. In time though, he was known as a great king in all the world, even though many people fought against him.

Suppressed identity simply put, is when we know what God wants us to do and others tell us no. These others can be friends, family, or even people from church.

The danger here is getting this mixed up with Denied Identity. If we ignore good counsel and continue to go after something we shouldn't go after, we claim that we are being suppressed. Again, we must stay in the Word of God in order to stay connected to the true source of wisdom.

If God is using someone to truly give us Godly advice, it will line up with what the Holy Spirit is already telling us. It will also line up with what we have been reading in the Bible. This means we must be reading the Bible.

The perfect verse in the Bible is found in the first half of the story of David.

1 Samuel 16:7
But the Lord said to Samuel, "Do not look at his appearance or his stature, because I have rejected him. Man does not see what the Lord sees, for man sees what is visible, but the Lord sees the heart." HCSB

This verse works for how people see us, and how we see ourselves. There are times we know that God has something special planned for us and others around us don't see it. This doesn't mean it is not true.

We can rest assured because God has everything under control. Repression from others cannot and will not stop God's plan for our lives. We must keep moving forward and not let others hold us back. Do what God has put in your heart and the plan that the Holy Spirit is leading you through.

Hebrews 10:36 (NLT)
Patient endurance is what you need now, so that you will continue to do God's will.

Questions:

1. Have you been affected by someone else's hate?
   _____

2. Has God given you a plan for your life that others have criticized?
   _____
   _____

3. What have you done through Christ that others have said No?
   _____
   _____
   _____

4. Are you waiting for a promise to be fulfilled?
   _____

5. What is the promise or work the Lord has for you to do that you are waiting for the final Go from God?
   _____
   _____

Jesus gave us the Holy Spirit to guide us. He wants to Guide you to an amazing future. You are worthy.

Thoughts:

Chapter 6

Hidden Identity

You have probably heard the phrase, 'Tapping into their hidden potential." This can be hidden in two different ways. One is when it is not seen by others, the other is when the person doesn't see it in themselves. This chapter will look at self-doubt. Even after we hear from God, we don't believe it.

This is a very common reaction throughout the Bible. It would be safe to say, most people doubted God when he called them. From the outside looking in, it seems ridiculous that anyone who gets an audible invitation from God Himself would tell Him they can't. Part of it is doubting God would really ask us to do anything and the other is not fully believing God wants us to succeed.

A great example of this is a man named Gideon. He lived in Israel before they had a king. The Midianites had taken over most of Israel and was oppressing the children of God. Gideon was a young man with no distinct skill. You can read the full story in Judges chapter six.

The Angel of the Lord came to talk to Gideon. It is very interesting that Gideon responded with a question that doesn't quite match what the Angel said.

Judges 6:12 & 13
Then the Angel of the Lord appeared to him and said: "The Lord is with YOU mighty warrior."
Gideon said to Him, "Please Sir, if the Lord is with US, why has all this happened?" HSCB

A lot is going on here. God calls Gideon a mighty warrior. God addresses Gideon directly with a compliment, and Gideon replies with a big fat us. It was as if he denied the compliment. Do you know someone like that, or are you like that?

He was also in disbelief that God cared about Israel. There had been many years since God had helped them. Gideon knew the stories of God's miracles. He had his doubts that God would help them again. He, like many, felt abandoned. In this case, God was going to use him to get back in action helping the Israelites.

God performs a miracle to show that he is from God. Then he puts Gideon to work tearing down the altar of Baal. But when it came to God directing him to go and fight against the Midianites, Gideon said whoa.

He said he was going to help, but just to make sure God really wanted him to lead the army, he needed a sign. The sign was impossible. The dew in the morning would made a fleece wet. But not the ground. The next morning it was so, but Gideon still wasn't convinced that he was the man for the job, so he asked God for another sign. This time he asked for the opposite. In the morning the fleece was dry, and the ground was wet.

Gideon gathered his men and prepared for war. As you can read in Judges 7, God whittled the army from 32,000 warriors to 10,000. God told Gideon there were still too many.

I think many of us have been there. God gives us a clear direction. Then once we say yes, He makes the path even harder.

God continued to eliminate warriors until there were only 300 left. That's right, he started with a grand army of 32,000, only to be left with 300. Long story short, God was with him and they chased the enemy out of the land.

Like Gideon, we can be asked to do something for God and feel like someone else would be better for the job. If this were true, God would have asked someone else. The best lesson is when Gideon finally agreed to God's request and didn't give up.

We can say yes and start the process, only to find out it is way harder than we thought it would be. When God calls us, he knows we have everything we need inside us, even if we do not see it for ourselves. As I have said before, willingness is 75% of what God is looking for. God already knows our weaknesses. He is totally prepared to strengthen our weaknesses and intervene at just the right time to help us win the battle.

God knows our weaknesses and knows our limits, but he also knows our strengths. Gideon wasn't a warrior by nature, so God handled most of the fighting, but he was a great leader. Gideon could rally the troops, literally. He was able to round up 32,000 people willing to fight. After God took out the Midianites, the people who originally questioned Gideon's abilities begged him to be their leader permanently.

Sometimes only God sees our hidden potential. When we allow God to draw it out of us, we can find ourselves in impossible situations. We also find ourselves accomplishing amazing things. Sometimes it is as a leader and sometimes we are simply one of the 300 that are still very active in the miracle. The impossible is possible when God calls us, and we go.

Jay Johnson - who I had the pleasure of singing with for many years has a great testimony. It ends with dropping to his knees in a hotel room and calling out to God. "I don't know why you would want someone like me, but if you will have me, I will play for you the rest of my life." That was in 1978 and he has kept his word. Jay gave up being a musician on the road performing with the top artists in the 70's to living for Jesus. Knowing him as I do, he says and lives as if he never regretted that prayer.

Let God draw out your hidden identity. God isn't going to set us up to fail. He may allow us to stumble or fail at a single task, but the end game is always for our benefit.

Jeremiah 29:11 (NLT)
"For I know the plans I have for you," says the Lord. "They are plans for good and not for disaster, to give you a future and a hope."

Questions:

1. Name some of the reasons God can't use you?

   _____
   _____
   _____

2. Name the hidden potential you feel inside but are afraid to tap into it?

   _____
   _____
   _____

3. What can you do to develop or unleash your potential?

   _____
   _____

Jesus can see the best in you even if it hast emerged yet. He wants to not only draw it out, but he wants to use it to help others. Let your faith in him push out the fear of failure.

Thoughts:

Chapter 7

Resented Identity

Resentment of identity is very common. It can happen with our dream identity as well as unwanted ones. Our identities can cause roadblocks in our lives. They can also block our humility.

Success can be a dream come true or the end of happiness. I think we all want to be successful. We also want our kids to be successful. The trouble is success by nature applies an identity to a person, leaving the person unable to remove the identity. This is very common with TV roles. The character's name becomes a household name, but no one knows the actor's real name. To America, the character is who they are. To emphasize this point, here are a few examples. See if you can think of their real name.

Barney Fife –
Luke Skywalker –
Joey Tribbiani –
Kramer –
Flo from Progressive –
Napoleon Dynamite –

People you would recognize in a second if seen on the street but would never remember their real name. So, you call from across the street, "Hey Kramer! How's Jerry?"

At first the attention is an amazing thing. But after a while, the fact no one knows their real identity can get them down. It leads to depression. It leads to an identity crisis. It isn't long after this point when the actor begins to resent the role. The very role that changed his life forever. The role that made him famous.

Much like musicians, they become one hit wonders. Sometimes they even get a spin off show, but it is still the same character. Kramer from the Seinfeld show was amazing on the show, but roles afterwards were few and far between. Radar from Mash, and many more became character actors. I could go on and list actors you may not know. This would partially prove my point. But think of someone from a show you loved as a kid and think about where they are now.

It is easy from our side to not understand. "How can they resent the role? Give me the role and they can call me anything they want." I know I have said it.

Being famous is very hard on an identity.

In the sixties, 4 young men were picked to be a fake rock band for a kid's comedy show. Their first song, which they sang themselves, went to number 1 on the charts. They were an overnight success. A number one hit song and they had never even sung together in front of a live audience. While this was happening, they were in the studio taping the TV show.

They were just about completely unknown to the world prior to the show airing for the first time. They had never set out to be rock stars, but there they were.

The Resented Identity came when word got out that they weren't playing the instruments. Should it have mattered? It was their voices on the 45's. And I can honestly say, I loved the results of their four voices. I didn't care who was playing the instruments.

I loved the show as well. Two of the four actually did play guitar and were not allowed to play. This drove them crazy and it caused a big riff on the set.

Here they were huge stars and upset because the producers wouldn't let them play their own instruments. I still don't get it fully. I do know pride makes all of us make unwise decisions.

They would eventually learn to play their own songs and do pretty well. But the resentment would cut the show short. I still watch it today: The Monkees.

Some of the hardest hit by fame is the kids. Life is great until they grow up. And many of us can feel the pain. They grow up, but America doesn't want them to grow up. Since they are not cartoons, the growth is unstoppable.

They suffer from type casting and the inability to get any roles at all. In some cases, the only jobs they can get is family films. Since they are teens or young adults, they want to be taken seriously. The Oscar never goes to the cute funny actors. Resentment leads to rebellion.

The end results usually end up with drugs and alcohol. For young men it is hard to break out of the shadow of the past. Young ladies sometimes shed all the cutesy kids' stuff by shedding their clothes. The resentment leads to the feelings of "I will prove I am not a kid anymore."

Today we know many that have struggled. Amanda Bynes, Macaulay Culkin, Jodie Sweetin, and so on. Some have turned around and have embraced their fans. But it has been very difficult for them.

Their wildest dreams have come true, but the cost was more than they were willing to pay.

Like I said, it isn't just a problem famous kids have. We all must prove ourselves. Parents don't trust us to be adults even though we are eighteen or nineteen. This can lead to resentment and family riffs.

This resentment can be throughout our lives. It can come from being identified by others differently than we want to be identified. work, family, church, or neighborhood.

It can happen when we are young or when we are old. Anytime that someone else projects an unwanted identity on us, it produces stressful result.

There is not a step by step way to handle this. Every situation is different, and only the Holy Spirit can lead you in how to properly deal with it. If we act in resentment, we will destroy relationships and end friendships. This is not acting out in love. In some cases, you need to do something to change this perception. In other cases, you need to accept it, because it is the identity that God wants you to embrace.

Uncovering our hidden identity can be complicated, but by the end of this book, I hope you will understand where you are and where you should be.

Psalms 20:4
May he give you what your heart desires and fulfill your whole purpose. HCSB

Questions:

1. Has God asked you to do something you regretted?

   _____

   _____

2. Have ever started a good work, which turned out differently than you had originally planned?

   _____

   _____

3. Can you think of a time when you joined a team and ended up with a task or job you didn't intend?

   _____

   _____

4. When has God done something unexpected and it turned out amazing?

   _____

   _____

The unexpected should be expected. Have faith the God who created you knows the perfect surprise to place you in the middle of a miracle.

Thoughts:

Chapter 8

Skeptical Identity

Some of the biggest tasks God has set before mankind were given to people who didn't think they could handle it.

In Exodus 3, we find Moses has killed an Egyptian and already fled for his life. He has been living in Midian as a shepherd. God is visiting him in the burning bush. This is where God tells Moses he is going to rescue the Israelites and lead them to Canaan the land flowing with milk and honey. Then God drops the bomb.

Exodus 3:10 (NLT)
"Now go, for I am sending you to Pharaoh. You must lead my people Israel out of Egypt."

Moses gave a shout and yelled, "Yes, finally! Let's go get them out of there!"

Wait. No, he didn't. He did the exact opposite.

Exodus 3:11 (NLT)
But Moses protested to God, "Who am I to appear before Pharaoh? Who am I to lead the people of Israel out of Egypt?"

In verse 12, God tells him he will be with him. Moses still isn't convinced. He asks God what he is supposed to say. This is where God calls himself the I AM. He also calls himself Yahweh.

Exodus 3 is an amazing chapter. It is a real conversation between a man with issues, and God. It is worth reading on your own. God has a lot more to tell Moses and there are a lot of memorable verses to remember.

Chapter 4 finds Moses still not going for it.

Exodus 4:1 (NLT)
But Moses protested again, "What if they won't believe me or listen to me? What if they say, 'The Lord never appeared to you'?"

God turns his staff into a snake and clears a disease. Finally, Moses was ready.

Exodus 4:10 (NLT)
But Moses pleaded with the Lord, "O Lord, I'm not very good with words. I never have been, and I'm not now, even though you have spoken to me. I get tongue-tied, and my words get tangled."

God tells him he will help him with that.

Exodus 4:13 (NLT)
But Moses again pleaded, "Lord, please! Send anyone else."

This made God mad, and He told him he could take Aaron with him.

No one argued with God more, or pleaded to God to change his mind more, than Moses.

Do you relate to how Moses felt? Even if we have been reluctant, even if we said no to our calling by God, even with very clear direction, we have said "No, thank you." Despite all this, it is not too late. We can say yes. Just like God helped Moses through every obstacle, He will help us.

HE WILL HELP YOU.

It is all part of our faith. If God calls us, we already have most of what we need and has a full supply of help for what we lack.

God's plans are not just the vague impressions that we can see or feel. The plan is complete, with every provision, help, and timing. For all the details we may find ourselves worrying about, God already has it covered in his plan.

We don't always see the plan. In fact, we rarely see how the plan is falling into place. God loves to include miracles and surprise guests within the plan.

If this is you, pray for wisdom and ask God to help you get started. Pray for faith to overpower skeptical thoughts. Then take that first step.

1 Corinthians 9:8 (NLT)
And God will generously provide ALL you need.

Questions:

1. What's your biggest insecurity?

   _____

   _____

2. Have you overcome an insecurity?

   _____

3. How were you blessed by it?

   _____

   _____

4. Has God provided a miracle when you needed it, to finish a task?

   _____

   _____

5. Do you believe God will provide the help and skills you need to be who he has called you to be?

   _____

God doesn't put you on a path to fail. Be brave and be bold. God will see you through.

Thoughts:

Chapter 9

Rejected Identity

The worst of all the identity crises is Rejected Identity. This is just as it sounds. It is when and if we just completely reject God's calling.

The most common reason for rejection is when God's plan isn't what we expected. God's plan is so often the opposite of what we want.

In this chapter, I want to look at Judas. He was not the obvious betrayer. Look at the night Jesus told the twelve disciples that one of them would betray him.

During the Last Supper, after Jesus washes the disciples' feet, he predicts his betrayal.

John 13:21-25 (NLT)

Now Jesus was deeply troubled, and he exclaimed, "I tell you the truth, one of you will betray me!" The disciples looked at each other, wondering whom he could mean. The disciple Jesus loved was sitting next to Jesus at the table. Peter motioned to him to ask, "Who's he talking about?"

In Mark, it says the disciples all asked, "Is it I?" Peter and John didn't know who it could be. The rest were hoping it would be themselves. There wasn't one that stood out as the one. This means no one suspected Judas. Up to this point, he was just as devoted as the rest.

Like many others, Judas was really expecting Jesus to come riding in on a white horse to save them all from the evil Roman Empire. Instead, Jesus spent his time declaring the real enemy was the Devil and not the people that hate them.

If it was me, I have no doubt I would be complaining and saying, "What about the Romans? When is he going to do something about the Romans? He keeps acting like the Pharisees are the bad guys. Come on! The Romans are the ones ruining everything."

I'm pretty sure I wouldn't have been one of the twelve.

While we don't know all the factors, it is a common thought that Judas got fed up with Jesus' inactivity. After Jesus started to predict His death, Judas decided to switch sides.

After over two years of training to change the world, Judas gave up. He rejected the calling of a disciple.

Whenever I tell the story of Judas, I always point out that he didn't do anything that Jesus wouldn't forgive. It is important for all of us to remember grace. Even if we deny, ignore, or reject God's calling, we can repent and return to God.

If Judas hadn't committed suicide, Jesus would have taken him back and he would have been part of the early church.

I know people who rejected the calling of God many years ago and are now in full time ministry. Sometimes what we think is a "too late" situation is actually God's perfect timing all along. God knows when we are going to move into action and when we aren't. There is no decision we make that surprises God.

Rejection is not good, but it isn't the end of it until life is up. There is still time to turn back to the path God has for us.

It isn't too late for forgiveness.

People have rejected their identity in Jesus because His plan is not what they wanted, and they didn't wait to see the end result.

Another reason some people reject what God has put on their heart is sin. Once we ask for forgiveness, Jesus makes us clean. The trouble is we sin again. Then we sin some more. We never get to the point of living a perfect life. We just continue to try. We continue to ask for forgiveness.

The trouble with this constant falling short of perfection, we can feel unworthy of a life and identity in God. The effect is rejecting the identity out of this feeling of unworthiness. It is easy to feel like we are less than everyone else at church. It is common to feel like someone or everyone else is more worthy. We saw this in the Moses story.

Truth is, God is not looking for perfect people; he is looking for willing people. He knows exactly what our weaknesses are. He knows our sin. He knows what we are not good at. He knows better than we know ourselves.

BUT he knows what we are good at. He knows the intentions of our heart. He knows our full potential. He knows the greatness within us. He knows exactly how He can use us for the plans He has for us and for others. Remember our plans are never just for our benefit. They are always to use us to help someone else.

Regarding the intentions of our heart, this may be the most important part next to our willingness. It is the measurement of our usability. Talent and potential are all well and good, unless they are unleashed within a person with evil intentions. If our intentions are for good, even if we fail in our daily lives from time to time, God can use us for good.

Ephesians 2:10 (NLT)
For we are God's Masterpiece. He has created us anew in Christ Jesus, so we can do the good thing he planned for us long ago.

If we fall short in our own eyes, we must remember how Jesus gives us righteousness through His blood. It is this righteousness that is given to us, not earned, that gives us the right and ability to live in our Best Identity.

We must stay humble acknowledging our sin and shortcomings, but then ask for forgiveness and move on. Accept the forgiveness of Jesus and put our eyes on back on Jesus and his plans for us. It is not too late if we have rejected God's plan.

Titus 3:5 (NLT)
He saved us, not because of the righteous things we have done, but because of his mercy. He washed away our sins, giving us a new birth and new life through the Holy Spirit.

Thoughts:

Chapter 10

Best Identity

It is OK to be you!

God isn't calling you to completely change you. He is calling you to use your uniqueness. He needs the **parts of you that are different**. He needs the hidden parts, the suppressed parts, and the skeptical parts.

Some of us will be called to huge and unbelievable tasks. Most of us will be called to simple tasks, like leading a small group, praying for someone, giving a helping hand, or providing comfort.

The common factor in whatever the task is, we must do it in faith and in LOVE. In everything we do, we must do it in love.

Hebrews 6:10 (NLT)
He will not forget how hard you have worked for him and how you have shown your love for him by caring for other believers. as you still do.

1 Corinthians 16:13-14 (NLT)
Be on guard. Stand firm in faith. Be courageous. Be strong. And do everything in love.

Embrace the calling and your God given identity. Live life to the fullest and don't be afraid to serve God in any way. Work within your personality and identity. But as Moses, we need to be willing to go places we are not comfortable with.

If God leads us to tasks that are not an exact match to how we see ourselves, believe God needs us within the task to reach someone no one else can.

When others try to talk you out of doing what God has called you to do, pray and go for it.

God is our provider.

God is the miracle worker.

God has the master plan.

God wants you to do amazing things.

God will not let you fail if you follow Him.

Our best identity is when we are just ourselves. Being who God has created us to be. Being the very person, we want to be deep down. Being the person that is kind, gentle, and willing to use our giftings to help others.

PURPOSE. What's our purpose and what are we going to do with our new identity? We all want to have a purpose. I believe we all do.

God has placed that purpose within our hearts. It is part of our desire to help others. It is also something called vision. Vision is how we see our future or the desire to do something in the future.

In order to grab hold of our best identity, we may need to drop an old identity that is preventing us from being our best: Angry, Partier, Liar, Lazy, or something hidden.

Becoming our best identity will take some reflection, prayer, and action. Once we identify our purpose it will take action to make it become real. It is very easy to know who we need to be and then do nothing to accomplish it. The actions we need to do may result in changing bad habits. It may also result in changing friends, changing jobs, or changing spending habits.

I pray that you understand what you are called to do. I hope you can now see who you are and who you can be. I pray that you are not afraid to act to get on the right path and open up your heart to embrace it.

Remember it may not be easy for you, but it will be amazing. The journey will be crazy, but it will also be filled with God's miracles and provision.

You **are** the one God needs to help someone.

You **are** the one God LOVES.

You **are** going to fulfill that vision that God has birthed inside of you.

Embrace your identity and never let anyone belittle it or you. Nothing is too small, and nothing is too big. God has your back.

Isaiah 42:6
I Yahweh, have called you for a purpose, and I will hold you by your hand. HCSB

Questions:

As we finish up, I want you to look at yourself.

1. What's the vision God has placed inside you?
   _____
   _____

2. What is the desire you have, to help others?

   Is it to help children, woman, teens, the hungry, the lost, the home bound, the sick, or the homeless?
   _____

3. How has the enemy held you back?
   _____
   _____

4. How have you held yourself back?
   _____
   _____

5. What is your Purpose?
   _____
   _____

6. What old identities do you need to release?

   _____

   _____

7. Who are you?

   _____

   _____

8. Who are you going to be?

   _____

   _____

Thoughts:

Made in the USA
Monee, IL
10 November 2020